Postman Panda

Authored and Illustrated by

Jessica LO

作者

TRANSNATIONAL PRESS LONDON

CHILDREN BOOKS: 05
Postman Panda
Authored and Illustrated by Jessica LO
作者
Jessica LO

First Published in 2024 by Transnational Press London in the United Kingdom, 13 Stamford Place, Sale, M33 3BT, UK.
www.tplondon.com

Transnational Press London® and the logo and its affiliated brands are registered trademarks.

Requests for permission to reproduce material from this work should be sent to: sales@tplondon.com

Paperback
ISBN: 978-1-80135-291-8
Digital
ISBN: 978-1-80135-292-5

Cover Design: Jessica Lo

Postman Panda

Jessica LO

作者

Jessica LO

1

One sunny morning,
there was a busy Panda spotted running
downtown.
This panda was known as ...

Postman Panda!

在一个阳光明媚的早晨，
一只忙碌的熊猫在市中心奔跑。
这只熊猫被称做…

熊猫邮递员！

2

**Postman Panda was not very kind to
other people
and did not treat them
how he would like to be treated.**

熊猫邮递员对其他人并不友好，

也没有想过，

如何像其他人对待他一样，

去对待他人！

5

**This Panda did not deliver letters
and parcels to FRONT doors.
He delivered them through the CHIMNEY.**

这只熊猫不把信件和包裹送到前门。

而是，通过高高的烟囱，投送信件和包裹。

6

HOME

MAIL

8

Postman Panda put his hat on
and got ready to deliver his first parcel.
He placed all the parcels and
letters in his bag.

熊猫邮递员戴上帽子，准备投递他的第一个包裹。

他把所有的包裹和信件都装进了他的包里。

9

Then, he started to notice the sun vanishing. The sky began to turn grey, and clouds began to darken, Postman Panda was stuck in the middle of a thunderstorm!

然后，他开始注意到太阳消失了。

天空开始变得灰暗，乌云密布，熊猫邮递员被困在了

雷雨之中！

10

Postman Panda heaved his way through the thunderstorm but no luck.
Parcels and letters started to get wet.

熊猫邮递员在雷雨中艰难地前行，但这一切，并不顺利。
包裹和信件开始被打湿。

12

After a while, the thunderstorm started to settle, and he could not find shelter.

过了一会儿，雷雨开始减弱，但他仍然找不到避雨的地方。

14

16

He felt hopeless.

他感到绝望

17

But he did not give up.

但是他没有放弃。

18

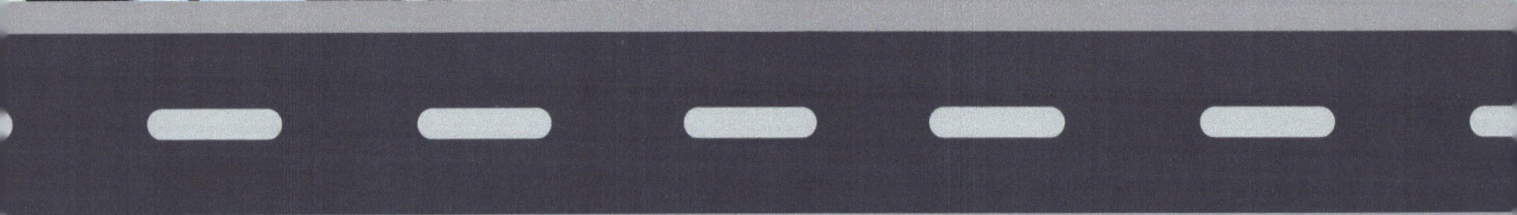

20

Postman Panda tried to find shelter throughout the town, but no one opened their FRONT doors to mean Postman Panda. He had run out of options.

熊猫邮递员试图在整个小镇上寻找避雨的场所，但是没有人愿意为这个吝啬的熊猫邮递员敞开 自家的前门。他别无选择。

The only choice left was to deliver at least ONE parcel to someone's FRONT door not CHIMNEY.

唯一的选择就是至少把一个包裹送到别人家的前门而不是烟囱门。

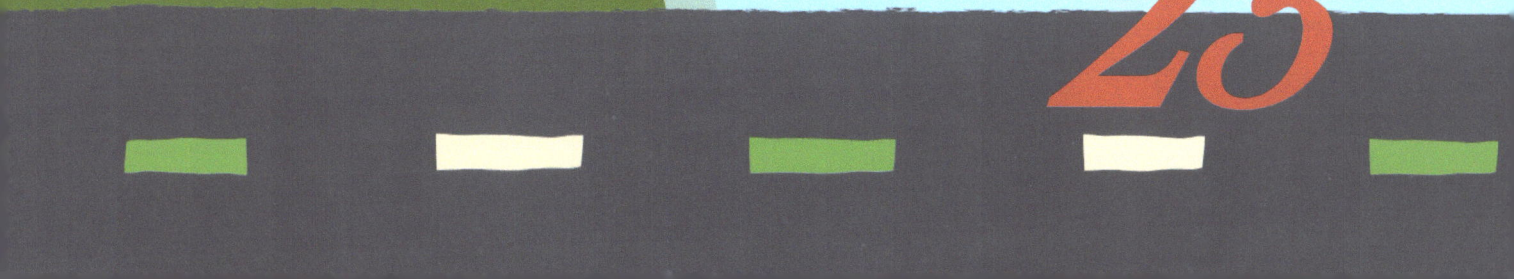

23

And to his relief, he successfully
delivered his first parcel through
the FRONT door
and luckily found shelter!

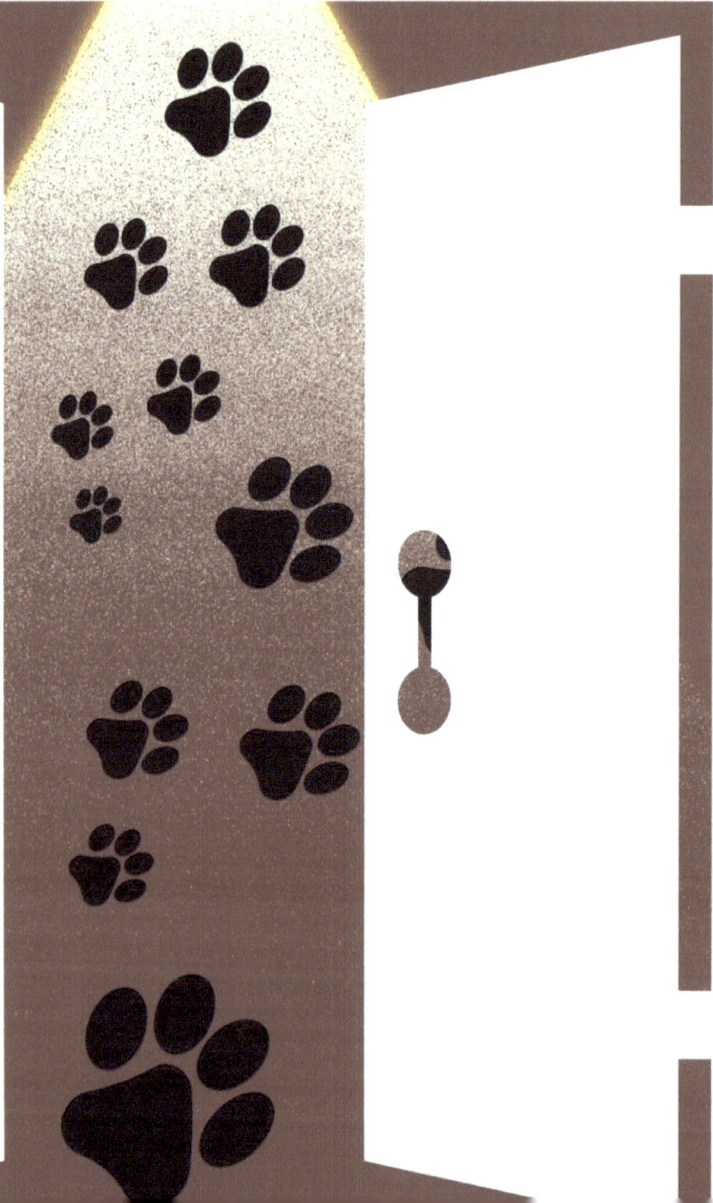

24

让他感到欣慰的是，他成功地从前门投递了第一个包裹，并幸运地找到了避雨的地方！

25

Surprisingly, he received a towel to dry him off, biscuits and hot tea to warm his body and the family's appreciation that he delivered the parcel in the thunderstorm.

出乎意料的是，他收到了主人家的毛巾，可以擦干身体；饼干和热茶，可以温暖身体，以及主人家对他在雷雨中投递包裹的感谢。

26

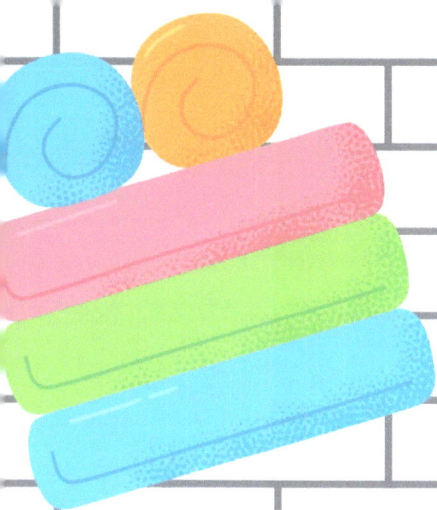

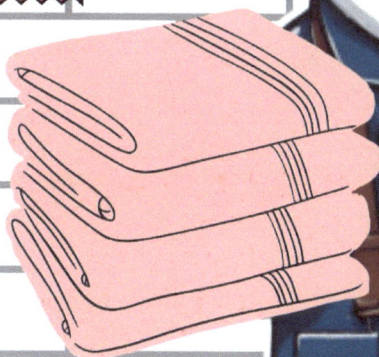

27

KINDNESS

28

The family that lived there had kindly given all their caring to the Postman Panda and finally they allowed him to stay there until the thunderstorm had stopped.

Postman Panda was overwhelmed by their kindness.

住在那里的一家人对熊猫邮递员给予了无微不至的关怀，最后他们允许熊猫邮递员呆在那里，直到雷雨停止。
熊猫邮递员被他们的好心感动了。

29

After that, Postman Panda discovered the true meaning of kindness and, of course, finished delivering all the parcels and letters to the town.

从那以后，熊猫邮递员发现了善良的真正含义，当然也完成了所有包裹和信件的投递工作。

30

www.ingramcontent.com/pod-product-compliance
Lightning Source LLC
Chambersburg PA
CBHW040916100426
42737CB00042B/99